Holding Pattern

Holding Pattern

Shane Rhodes

© Copyright Shane Rhodes 2002

All rights reserved. The use of any part of this publication reproduced, transmitted in any form or by any means, electronic, mechanical, recording or otherwise, or stored in a retrieval system, without the prior consent of the publisher is an infringement of the copyright law. In the case of photocopying or other reprographic copying of the material, a licence must be obtained from the Canadian Reprography Collective before proceeding.

Canadian Cataloguing in Publication Data
Rhodes, Shane, 1973-
Holding pattern
Poems.
ISBN 1-896300-60-X

I. Title.
PS8585.H568H64 2002   C811'.6 C2001-911661-6
PR9199.3.R4643H64 2002--

Editor for the Press: Douglas Barbour
Cover image: Mike Reichert Steinhauer
Cover and interior design: Ruth Linka
Author photo: Rob Rhodes

   Canadian Patrimoine
Heritage canadien

NeWest Press acknowledges the support of the Canada Council for the Arts and the Alberta Foundation for the Arts for our publishing program. We also acknowledge the financial support of the Government of Canada through the Book Publishing Industry Development Program (BPIDP) for our publishing activities.

Some of these poems have appeared in: *Alberta Views, Arc, Ariel, Canadian Literature, filling Station, Grain, Greenboathouse Books, Prairie Fire, Qwerty, The Fiddlehead* and *The Malahat Review*. "Stuff" was commissioned and broadcast by CBC Radio's *Definitely Not the Opera*. "Clutch" was originally published as a chapbook by House Press.

Acknowledgements: I would like to thank Douglas Barbour and the people at NeWest Press for all their help and editing suggestions. I would also like to thank to all those who read and helped this manuscript in progress. Both the Canada Council for the Arts and the Alberta Foundation for the Arts provided financial support during the completion of this book.

NeWest Press
201–8540–109 Street
Edmonton, Alberta
T6G 1E6
(780) 432-9427
www.newestpress.com

1 2 3 4 5 06 05 04 03 02

PRINTED AND BOUND IN CANADA

"a time to think of everything the earth
and I had lost, of all
                    that I would lose,
of all that I was losing."

> Agha Shahid Ali
> *A Nostalgist's Map of America*

Contents

I
    Night Storms ∽ 2
    Driving ∽ 7
    Talking About it with Andrew ∽ 9
    Sidereal Time ∽ 11
    In the Past Tense ∽ 13
    Listening ∽ 15
    Potatoes ∽ 17
    Fucking ∽ 19
    Stuff ∽ 20
    Still Life with Apple ∽ 22
    Return of the Hunters ∽ 23
    Rivers
        Lundeen ∽ 25
        Skookumchuk ∽ 26
    Mountains ∽ 27
    The Captive ∽ 29

II   Clutch
    Play the Pipes Lowly and Play the Pipe Slowly ∽ 34
    D'Accord, Baby ∽ 35
    Roots ∽ 36
    What are you Doing Tonight? ∽ 37
    A Woman in a Lace-up Maple Leafs Hockey Sweater Can
        Be a Beautiful Thing ∽ 38
    Just This One Last Time, I Promise ∽ 39
    Are You Okay Down There? ∽ 40
    His Hands Were Hounds Over Me ∽ 41
    Lucky ∽ 42
    Tea in the Morning is So Civilized ∽ 43
    Poker-Face ∽ 44
    10% ∽ 45
    In This Damn Town, Even the Moon is New ∽ 46

Just This One Last Time, I Promise ～ 47
Stolen Time ～ 48
Let the Horse Wander ～ 49
One Good Draft Would Finish Him ～ 50
Fetish ～ 51
He Waits Until Tomorrow ～ 52
There is an Obvious Solution to Your Problem ～ 53
Madame Marie Curie ～ 54
I Have Done This to Show What an Englishman Can Do ～ 55
No, This is Not the Bat Cave ～ 56
The End of This Section ～ 57

III
Day and Night the Sea Whispered Thalassa ～ 60
Daybreak on 5th Street ～ 63
A Letter ～ 65
In the Museum ～ 67
Desires for Symmetry ～ 70
Embodiment ～ 71
In the Beginning, Pornography ～ 73
Steam ～ 75
Tiger Lilies ～ 78
Les Jeunes Filles Cueillent Les Fleurs ～ 80
Octubre ～ 82
Meditation on the Butterfly Sanctuary ～ 84
Meditation on The Orchid Sanctuary ～ 85
Moth Light ～ 86
Pieces ～ 88

IV holding pattern ～ 91

Author biography ～ 104

I

Night Storms

Night in the trees, each gust of wind
turns them silver. It could be the end
of colour and small consequence.
My grandfather's pocket-watch, hanging
on the bookshelf, has begun to tick.
I remember the old man reaching into his pocket
saying "Here, kid, take this" and handing it to me.
It burnt cool in my hand
the way uranium is supposed to.
For how many years has it been stopped
the second hand drawn on that space
between four and five? For how long
the untallied air skimmed its surface?

A man sleeps in the next room
beneath flannel sheets. In this dark,
there is no room for him. All is crowded
by the cold breath of rain. All is ticking.
Family stories, friends I can't remember
but some part of me can't forget,
even those pieces sworn to the past
hotdrawn from the coagulated gears.
Down the dark halls, abandoned stairwells,
their footprints through the wet shagged grass
they come.

Great-grandmother who sailed from England
on a navy ship at the war's end (*the last war*,
they called it, believing there could be no other).
Six kids, five hundred men and pregnant
heaving her sickness over the gunwale.

She knew the Atlantic's long hyphen too well
and would never touch the sea again.
There may have been a prairie train station
at which she met her husband
who arrived 7 months before (did he carry
the ticking in his head?) though, just as probable,
there was only grassland and a thin scar
of tracks. It was summer. Her belly swelled
with a travelling birth.

My grandmother was six then.
When I knew her, she cooked in a rectory
for priests. They loved her, with their cassocks
and old skin, the way I did:
for she smelled like dogs in sleep
for the upturned carriage of her hips
for she killed chickens by hand
and coaxed pastry, unblemished, from flour.

Her husband complained daily
how he missed his first wife, dead
from childbirth. He was losing his mind
and spent days in a chair by the highway
counting cars and would buy each week
cases of lettuce for the rabbits that lived with them.
His only wish—that someone would put a hole in him.
Hoping for death, he lived long and peaceful
to the end.
                        (My grandmother
sat in the car, still angry after twenty years apart,
his body finally lowered beneath dirt.)

Memories echo around me
the way a voice carries in an empty room.

And I can hear the watch, still ticking,
still carrying it forward in continuous arrival
on the platter of its brass watch-face
propellering us through these type-faced years.
Father who drank himself to death at 34
(not much older than me) and stepped back
from the visible. Stepfather
electrocuted working seismic at 23,
the electricity still in his mangled hands.

When great-grandmother's husband died
(she outlasted two)
she married one of her boarders
(14 years younger)
and proceeded to have
(she was forty)
another family
(seven kids)
before he died too.

And why are we never smart enough
to ask our questions before their minds go
crazy with age? Grandmother in the nursing home
lost in whatever eternity saves or gives
or refuses, finally, to take away.
We'd get midnight complaints
from the orderlies. She wandered
the halls at night and slept with the men.
She spoke in wool sweaters and afghans
each year the colours more varied,
small pieces awkwardly woven, nothing
wasted. She believed she was poor again.
She believed she was moving to the city.
Every night she would pack

what the nurses in the day had unpacked—
celery and light bulbs wrapped in stockings.

The watch, buoyant in the night air,
organizes this small confluence of space.
Made in Canada it says to no one
in particular or only those interested enough
to pop off its back and (unlock the mysteries, etc.)
listen. It's the remittance of everything we need.
"Here, kid, take this"—for what else could he do
but give the thing away
just as we will give ourselves away
to whoever, in the end, will take us.

My other grandmother's story:
just after the turn of the century
and the only thermometer for three hundred miles
was owned by a family outside of town.
Everyday the schoolmistress would call
(on the only telephone?)
and ask the temperature
which she would pass on
to the children in the morning
who would pass it on
to their parents in the afternoon
who would pass it on
to their neighbours at night.
Information spreading its own
slow storm-front. It was the end of words
giving name to weather.
So cold, she would say, *the air cracked
when you breathed. So cold
even the watches stopped ticking.*

(A story
I must pass on for I am like my grandmother,
human, and trapped in the telling.)

      The man in the next room
moans in his sleep and the house answers
with silent words of its own. The wind is out there
you can see its study on each poplar leaf.
My mind mulls over its night catch:
stories, scars, what we carry forward
in our mangled hands. These lives
dissolved to their thinnest details
and the unclotting stroke
of a second hand.

Driving

Two thousand miles and you
and I are driving through the prairies,
driving to the east coast through these
small words and endless repetitions of space.
The pavement splayed through fields
as if, too, feeling its limits.
Stations on the radio surface in and
out of static, the music of this place—
wheat baking in summer thermals,
barley at the side of the road bends
in our wake. In this bruised light,
you sleep and we could be nothing
but the chronicles of our escapes—
always surprised by what we loved
by what chose to love us.
If we spoke, what would we say?
Something full of longing
but empty of appetite?
An insight from the radio gospel hour
or *Bargain Finder* where someone
gets closer to god while someone else
sells a tractor? *There is something I want*
and the more I enter it the more I need
to enter. At a laboratory in CERN
(the radio news now) they have discovered
a new type of matter—something smaller
than smallest—while we, on a road
in northern Nebraska, have found
the oldest type of space. There is no end
to what we run away from or to.
Even together we were more singular

than alone. *Praise be to god* the scientists
croon as they chain-link the world.
Poplars by the side of the road
fall into their name.
We will disappear then, too,
like matter, into the history
of our complaints.

Talking About it with Andrew

He told the most improbable stories.
Within a week, he would bring you
blurred pictures,
the "actual" knife.
One story of a friend
who joined the Foreign Legion.
After three days foodless,
a crate of chickens. "Supper,"
the Sergeant yelled opening
the crate to crazed chicken flight,
"Come and get it!"
No knives, no fire—just hands, teeth
and a hit of acid.

He had lived all his life there
in Fredericton or once for a year
in St. John. His travels never ranging far
from the smell of the river.
He worked a bit, went to school a bit,
sold a bit of hash. His father
the forestry's first entomologist: *"Son,
bugs are our bread and butter."*

On my last trip to the Bay of Fundy,
Andrew, driving his father's Buick,
described each type of tree we passed
with scientific exactness. He described them
as I'm sure his father had—
each with attached story.
Oak. Beech. King's Arrow Pine
named for the marks sailors gave them
so they could be used as masts

for the king's ships.

In the novels I have read
characters fill back pages
with a sadness of lost intent—
something about the end of plot
and being led on by need.
The hero by default
because her actions were necessary
and she knew no better.
Or the murderer moves us
because he has form in his anger.
We would sit, Andrew and I,
growing listless in the bug-clogged air
as the problems of books
became our own.

His first experiment with LSD:
he locked himself in a room
and came out a day and a half later
hands shaking, body drained,
a chemical grin on his face—mind caught
by the lustre of a new balance.

But what I remember most
those days and nights
of constant talk, his thin
wired body and a porch lit
by cigarettes and match light.

Sidereal Time

As stars etch their patterns
through the cloud chambers
of your eyes, the shock of being
in the world wears off
in concentric pairings.
The scent of night-flowering cactus
walks through the room as we sleep
while some cat coagulates darkness
and begins a private life.

Between the couch and lamp,
a spider, its web through the night
like an idea through space, so pure
it is nothing but a history of passage,
a thin line of grief holding—steadfast
and heavy—a night in the 21st century.
The moon, through the window's
melted hourglass sand, stalls
in its fine fibres.
The truth now not what we see
but what resists us, what surfaces
surface to guide us—if only as anchorage
—to morning. I think of how I watched us
in the mirror, working hard at the lines
between us and it seemed
I was watching strangers
whose forms laboured to merge. And
the spider, trying—
length
after length—
to make sense of it all

binding these spines through the air.
And we sleep in the cool silence after
as the liquids in our bodies
mix and combine. We sleep
pressed together inhaling
each other's breath as if night
might puncture the gaps between us.
The spider practices
only what it knows
this thin constellation
and its relation to the world.
To the *movable* world
where—all night—we are
connected.

In the Past Tense

Two uncles are not talking—
their glasses full of rye, ice
disappearing across the counter—
of the relative unlikeliness of the Holocaust
at a kitchen table in Alberta
far from the nearest fact
which winks amongst the shade.
Bones in dark loam melt
into new forests whose leaves,
aspen and poplar, carry the signs
of leaves.

In this story, there is no woman,
her skirt tied around her neck,
face, still beautiful and flushed,
pierced by a wound
that hangs above her eye.
She is not pulled into a world of men
where this is intended. And no one
with a gun looks shyly away—
buttoning his fly, legs bloody and wet
with urine—from the mess he has not made
of her. Already he remembers nothing:
for example, the trees, willow and birch,
how they could have crowded him
leaves like bruised eyeless lids.
Or the instant inutility of her body.
He remembers, as if precision
in darkness will matter, it was
not-autumn.

In a father's sock drawer
in the dark loam of cotton
two belt buckles with swastikas and eagles
endure a future they could not have imagined.
Pulled from the dead
by the dead relative who killed them
now scented with soap and cedar.
He must have touched these every day
as if memory were a muscle
kept strong by use.

And who will tell the stories
and what stories will they tell us
when even the relics gain new intention
and intention gains new weight.
And I remember how, on television one night,
they brought fish from deep water
into a boat and in our room
I heard—getting up to leave—
their small screams and—turning—
watched them explode on the screen.

In this story, something behind us
forever ascends. In this story,
there is a girl lost in the caves
where the bodies will never shut up.
In this story, Euridice keeps climbing
feet bruised on the disappearing rock steps.
She has books with her
where indelible things are written.
In this story, we are going to meet her.
The only words we carry
are these.

Listening

Someone plays Shubert in a house not far from here.
You can, when the wind is right, hear it leaking
beneath a kitchen window. Someone tries, bar
by bar, somebody else's idea of pleasure.
The notes fought a long way to get here
to this half mile away sitting by the side of the field
watching the grass darken with each gust of wind,
listening. One by one, out of the wound wires,
pedals and popping valves of their making,
out of the pillowed hammers, levers, and momentary finger
strokes, past the sleeping birches and dogs that pace nervously
with every off-note and some have been lost in the junk
piles of abandoned chain links, broken cultivator shanks
and much cobwebbed cabs of (barely visible
in the corroding twilight) Studebakers, 461 Cockshut Combines,
box springs, flat tires and one empty "Drink Bob's for Thirst"
soda bottle, Swift Current, circa 1939. They have come,
together then, still holding the fine line of melody
though a distant one, one strained of eloquence
sounding more like the sinewy calves of music
than its plump forethought. But they have come,
together, through so much detritus of human living
there is something human to them, they smell
like us, of use and over use, of debt and mediocre riches
not of Viennese parlours or a short fat man everyone called
The Mushroom, no, not of that but of small-town coffee shops,
of cigarettes and damp denim, of baseball caps saying to no one
in particular: Agricore, Bashaw Meats, Home Hardware. "Schubert,"
a part of me asks the other part that listens, "here?"
Or they die out between the geometry of octaves and 1/4
sections, the notes falling from the wires of harmony to the fall-worn

fields with no accompaniment but the quiet hum of silence
because they are so tired of noise and its platitudes, of melody and its
unending inventiveness, are so tired of it all and have travelled
so far to find themselves here in the middle of the one measure
they were trying so hard to escape. But they have done it,
and all they can do, now, is die, however tragically, however
("no one," hand across forehead, dust rising from each fallen note,
"is listening") wasted, beneath the night sleep
of randomness, beneath these stars rowing over us,
beneath all we have carried forward and dropped
along the way to get here.

Potatoes

Talk about silence
in silence.

My grandmother's face
when she talked of potatoes—
her eyes filled with the mineral thrill
of something she could grow a family on.
Her garden, once the site of a garbage dump.
In the spring, the dirt gave up
secrets of trash: ancient coke bottles,
key rings, boots, one glass eye.
In the fall, haemorrhoidal mounds
of potatoes, those red planets
orbiting the dark loam.

Garden glands, dirt
nodes, Jacques Cousteauvian
earth bubbles, the softer
deities of summer. Their names
cool the tongue: yukon gold,
russet, netted gem.

The elderly Hutterite man
trying to sell me everything
as we shuffle through the cold root-cellar
frost gleaming in the rafters.
"You want onions, I got onions, you want garlic, it's expensive stuff,
eggs, you want eggs, the egg ladies got eggs and slippers, my girls
been makin' slippers all fall, cheap cheap ten years guaranteed, say,"
he says, turning to me, his blind eyes tuber white, "you want some
slippers with these potatoes?"

    Dear Sally,
        Here they bury you with your eyes open. Send
        train fare.
            Love, Sal

They should fasten
    thirstily onto love
        and bury it
far within said Virgil
    but not of
  potatoes.

Fucking

How it was really our need we were decorating
and nothing else. The condom in my hand
everything physical and comedic   an oddity.
Twice it leapt from my hands gliding
through the air in perfect jellyfish oscillations.
My hands, covered with lube and bed lint,
scrambled for it as if it were, just then,
the very edge of both our lives.

And then it was on and we clunked
against each other's hard edges
in our closest approximation of sex.
The thing between us for we believed it
the truest point of passion and everything else
preparation. Pure lubricated fulcrum
of our rocking—holding us back and pushing
us forward. It was probably a Trojan
and I imagine poor Troy in its unbreachable walls
wooden horse covered with a sheet of latex
                        ("ultra sensitive") ("for your pleasure")
thirty Greeks beating the door trying to get out
lungs full of nonoxynol-9 or astroglide.
The horse rocking through the night
to their blue deaththroes.

This technology of withholding
our selves, what stops us from going too far
into each other. And then both of us
ridged as something outside us
wrenched the last juices out—
The walls of Troy unfallen
and unburned. Another piece
of the future slipped by
unproved.

Stuff

There are deals here no one has seen
discount rack mark ups mark downs   I am
a marked man here   I am therefore
I buy   in the forgotten aisles of men's
lady's wear and lady's men's wear you'll find
rare paintings of dogs playing pool   Boys
2 Men in ripped Calvin Klein jeans and
plastic boxes in plastic-wrapped paper bags
where you can lose the things that
organize your life   monitors play
the archaeology of TV   Michael Jackson
in "Thriller"   Bush before congress
the bombing of the middle east
beside video games where you can
bomb the middle east
                        And just where is the beef
and who in this mall will find it   and who
will just do it   think different   be whatever
they can be and feel part of the five billion
served   cooling under the heat-lamps
of appetite

Like a shirt on a discount rack, I just want
to be free.

                Minivans line the parking lot
like small domestic tanks   they have been driving
excitement for years   their arteries leak oil
of precambrian forests

                "Who wants to be a millionaire?"

someone asks someone else who answers, "Who wants
to be middle class and on credit?"

Temple of choice landfill of brand
name with so much to choose from
and everything still the same   please
tell me again how my satisfaction is always
guaranteed   how in the land of the free
the lowest price is the only law I'll need

I dream of walking the dark shopping aisles
by night   lit by fluorescent stripes
of running shoes and neon signs—
this is everything we make
and it makes us
and what will we be
come morning

Still Life with Apple

There is an apple on the counter
by the telephone.

There are no messages. If anyone calls
they will not, I think, get through.

If there is light through the window
it is morning, if not, evening.

If there is noise, it is the sound
of noise. No lights blink.

No electronic whistles.
Nothing calls for our attention.

The apple sits in this crust of air.
There are so many ends to green

when even light gives up on colour.
Something about it says it was picked

by hand and placed in tubs with russets
and spartans. Something about it falls

with the weight of rock in mountain passes
rock that takes three days to push away

and on the third it snows
and they let the cars through.

Cold flesh and bruised light.
Even here no one talks

of death or a family's slow
twistings in the air, only why,

in autumn, before snow,
the mind is so held

by fruit.

Return of the Hunters

Five o'clock and it feels too early
to name anything yet.
Trees soaked in silver frost.
Cold traces everything
with its equations. *Has to hurt
a little*, it thinks, *to be real,
to be sane.* The truck my father started
puffs a small fuselage of fire.

The stubbled wheat field we drive to
laid with plastic geese
in varying degrees of decay.
Hard to believe in a trick so simple but,
from far enough up, you suppose
everything looks like life or some
part of it—enough to make you believe,
as the flocks wheel over the fields,
they need this as much as we do.
                          The hunters,
stuffed in down-filled parkas and red hats,
behind their blinds practice calls.
Everything they don't know is out there
just beyond the reach of guns.
By the end of morning
they should know a bit more
especially those soft parts
with iridescent wings that fall,
wounded, through the trees.

The dogs whine in their cages
for it is their empire and they know
something will happen soon.
In the distance, flocks rise
like steam from the river.
My father puts his hand
on the back of my neck.
The hunters fumble
the last of their cigarettes.

Rivers

1. Lundeen

We hiked most the day to get there.
Through muskeg, swamps,
directionless paths, overgrown cut lines.
Stopped once to drink spring water
so cold it burned like alcohol.
By noon we were casting
our lines onto the Lundeen
which leads into Trout
where we camped the year before
(and had watched a moose break
from the postcard of its being
and trip, head first, into the creek)
then to Ram (which had run muddy
and unfishable all year).
Grass pulsed in the thick current.
The canvas vest you wore,
perforated with rusting hooks
ritual spinners and lures,
smelled of mildew and use.
Fish gills and fresh wounds gaped
in the shaken air.
An afternoon of small deaths:
trout in butter, lemon, campfire soot.
I write this as one living
in a city would write it,
with an open window
and a captured sense of pleasure.
Cars are my cool water.
You say a logging company

has clearcut a road to the creek
the halfday hike now driven.
Cellophane and cigarette butts
gather in the drying grass.

2. Skookumchuck

We camped so close to the river
our nights filled with the sound of rapids
as snowpack in the Kootenays melted
with record heat. The crash of falls
a half mile upstream echoed
from granite and shale.
We sunned ourselves
on the large midriver rocks
and stepped, hip-deep,
into the rising current.

The mornings may or may not have been
pleasant and I have no memory
to say we did not share with each other
our terrible moods. The bear we saw
surge of black across the road
may have been the image this memory
most clings to. Or you naked
on the green rocks.
                       Such heat
in those windless valleys, snow
between the spruce and poplar scrub.
Such heat and such scent of smoke
all over you.

Mountains

Most of your life lived in movies
b grade ninja films about assassins
with broken english and swaying morals
who barrel-rolled through highrise windows
opportunely placed skylights
to the applause of machine gun fire.
Death came quickly to the easily confused.

You made throwing stars from swather blades
nunchucks from hockey sticks and dog chains
even convinced your mother to sew you a ninja suit.
You assassinated the innocent pigs
harassed the tired Jersey cow
jumped from the highrise windows
of barn lofts to the unsuspecting
pigeons.

We went to scout camp together
(it was a small town, we were boys)
and one night you convinced me
to hike the mountain across the river
where we would stay the night and hike back
come morning. We were scared, every tree
hiding bear marks, but morning sunrise
echoed like a long shout over the mountains
and made all description insufficient.
We hiked back in silence.

Five years later, the car you drove
flipped into the soft ditch grass
(brome, crested wheat, barley)

three miles from your parent's home.
Your friend crawled with a broken back
to the nearest farm while you lay
beneath the cooling manifold.

Little else I can bring to your memory
other than the scraps of living. Your mother,
they say, still visits the grave every week.
The friend you were with addicted to heroin.
These are the scraps I assemble
under your name. Soon someone will look
at the photograph of a boy in black pajamas
looking action-figure sinister.
They will look, blankly,
and turn the page.

The Captive
for Boyd Schwartz

Taking off, the ground recedes from texture
into form again, lines (from this height already)
resume their curves and the small answers to direction.
Above the clouds, everything (plane, plastic window,
Colorado, a small wrapped container of cereal) swirled
into something the eye was surprised to create.
Sorrow. Yes, then, sorrow. Tears.
In my headphones, the captain's voice fades
to the start of strings and piano keys and with each
measure the ground below grows, like noise, uncontainable,
to what the heart must feel chasing its unending tail of blood.
Stravinsky and packaged milk. Music in the headphones
and tears moving in similar vectors of depression—
one through time, the other through space with you there
as you drive back (airport in the mirrors) to your parents,
mountains in the windshield holding down the edges.
At one time we were sure, but now . . . but now . . .
Everything rushing in to replace the named part
left us in the leaving. A cleft that, sitting here,
now listening, now crying to the classical channel,
now watching the movie just started on the overhead screens,
now looking out the window at the disappearing landscape
(Colorado, Wyoming, moving north along the continental divide),
some part of me was trying to fill with whatever it could.
Each piece of the plane humming, finding
in randomness its own piece of lust—which moved
at the speed of the girl on the TV screen
smiling for she is in love and moving (look out the window)
at just under the speed of light. But who can hear her
over the hum and click of the real.
Stewardesses smile, dumbly, for this game

they have played often. The small distance outside
the monitor screen cut with dust motes and light
through the windows (Montana). This moment,
(her hand by the closet door) (jump cut to her face)
has no history, no memory. You getting out of the car
900 miles away and tears (yes sorrow)
streaming at how many frames per second down your face.
Because this is only the beginning of the terrible.
Is this it, then, the tears telling us our edges?
Is this (what else will we have to ask for?)
what we have tried so hard to share, a small piece
of the light's misery? Alberta.
The boy in the movie kisses the girl
for it is the end of their country (the greatest ... etc.)
and the start of mine. Unending engines take me there.
You lean against the door and the earth comes
to take back what it had started with us, this
distance through stark valleys where the light stands
like wheat, where something lives and something,
however terrified and terrifying, is flying.

II

Clutch

"He stretched out his hand and from the shell I heard the long poem of the world."

Jeanette Winterson
Art and Lies

Play the Pipes Lowly and Play the Pipe Slowly

April is the cruellest month, the heart's weakest season, when it is too easily speared. Men walk shirtless in the warming air. A tough month with you[1] so far away. Come closer. No wonder men at sea become pirates, there is a meanness absence in abundance brings out. A longing with no attachment, no anchor. Moby Dick took down the whole ship—poor whale, poor Ahab. Sometimes all you have to love is hate. Sometimes all you have is a harpoon and sixty tons of flesh to drag you down.

˷

---

[1] I will call you Felice, girlfriend to Kafka, for happiness must be named, somewhere.

D'Accord, Baby

Giotto puts down his pen. He has had enough today. The Campanile has proved more difficult than he ever imagined. 1336, a year before his death, and he knows it. Soon the cathedral will be handed off to Talenti as it was handed to him from Arnolfo. The Campanile will be finished, he is sure, by Pisano. He thinks himself an unfortunate man of details; few things will take his name but he thinks yes, maybe, someday, he will be attached to the Campanile adding filler to a 1966 guidebook purchased by a priest's brother and given by the priest (beside a catalogue advertising Monk Brand Famous Incense ["Your incense has worked wonders! Ever since changing brands, my congregation has not once complained of nausea!"]) to me. But it is late in the morning, 1966, and seven years before my birth. The man who writes guidebooks is fretful. Summer and everything is art again and life is unmaintainable. He jots in his scribbler: "The rain was as cold as tears from Felice." He tries to sleep but it is so late. On the table beside him, a guidebook to Florence in which there are no women.

Roots

Spring makes winter terrible, every hollow aches for green. In Emily Dickinson's letters, someone has gone through and scratched out the name of her sister-in-law wherever it appears. No editor will hazard a guess as to why. Spring and I want to get lost in the superficiality of things. I want every attraction to hurt a little. September, 1910, and Franz Kafka writes in his diary, "I can't endure worry, and perhaps have been created expressly in order to die of it." He feels sick. He feels the way Kafka would feel with a headache. He wishes to flee the country by train. He wishes to be moved to the front. He wishes for the sound of a necklace being laid on a bedside table.

What Are You Doing Tonight?

Felice calls to tell me it will be another two months before we meet. Since when did I let a name get so close to me? Him, you, her, me—one by one we leave the body and chase it in language. Absence is the presence of repetition and repetition, the grammarians tell us, is the beginning of death. I wake, I eat, I sleep, I write with unfailing regularity. It kills me. It will spend the rest of my life killing me.

A Woman in a Lace-up Maple Leafs Hockey Sweater Can Be a Beautiful Thing

She sells books for a living but, in the end, who doesn't? She would go to Vancouver but the air there is too thick with the scent of men in shorts. The limit of my want is the air described by the area of her chest, the night-flex of ribs beneath cotton. If only I could make words like that, ones which cry out in the air as kids do in spring. But there is a bareness no luxury succumbs to—which means: every escape is partial—which means: the heart uncoils its blood like a rope. But the light gathers its tricks and card games. She shows me to the section entitled "Current Affairs" and I know, at least, she is willing. In hard times, there will be singing of hard times; even amongst friends, we will talk of being alone. The Canadians, incidentally, have fared poorly this year but it is a failure she has small responsibility to. Her thin, veined hand takes a book from the shelf, making it come, that much quicker.

Just This One Last Time, I Promise

Emily Dickinson was fascinated by the moment before death. As a child, her parents found it necessary to send her away for a month "after Emily had been permitted to witness for a few moments, at her own insistence, the approaching death of a girl of her own age." This need to see death intensified in the last decade of her life. About James D. Clark, she writes his brother in 1883: "I hope he was able to speak with you in his closing moment . . . I am eager to know all you may tell me of those final Days." She writes William S. Jackson soon after the death of his wife: "If you will tell me a very little of her Life's close?" Little written of the circumstances of her own death—sister-in-law finding the body and later the boxes of poems beneath her bed. A friend tells me of waking from sleep unable to move. She felt something on the bed beside her. Then a shadow on the ceiling pushing towards the open window. As it left, she could stir again. She could cry out. But she lay there, silent, as sweat pooled in the hollows of her body.

Are You Okay Down There?

Scaffolds of flesh.
Mud coils.
Turbulent brown rivers through rice paddies in China.
How many Mongols died to find the perfect horse crushing the sky in its gallop to heaven?
The favoured method of torture: wrap your enemy in carpet, trample on horseback.
Some riders not even dismounting to defecate but "deftly swinging their arses to the side."

My pretty.
My swift one.

His Hands Were Hounds Over Me

I think back to when we met. Our bodies were younger then and sex moved through our cells like heat from an acid etch. It still brings me to my knees. The only thing we didn't know of love was the magnitude of its disappointment. But I don't care anymore or, rather, believe at one time I cared. Nowadays, I sit in bars drinking beer as warm as the urine I pump out. I talk often. I put money in the jukebox and hear him rolling down the narrow passage. I try not to lose my head. I try to be with men who are normal which means I spend much of the night alone. I am so alone. I am torn asunder. My head floats beneath the darkening water.

Lucky

Moonlight.
White walls.

A drop of cum
on your cheek.

˞

Tea in the Morning is so Civilized

Miniature croissants the size of curled toes. Marmalade. Her grandmother spoke little English and I spoke little French. We knew each other in the civil distance between *bonjour* and *bien*. "Montréal is thesaurus for the lonely," she said. "Men in shirtsleeves leaning out of windows, smoke curdling in the air." Behind her apartment, men with walkers sat beside a pond with clipped-winged swans. As she started to lose her mind, she saw the neighbours sinking through the heat vents. But I remember those days, coming and going, always to find my need in a different pose of ease. It fit the palm of my habit. But she was so old. She was so tired of consoling and being consoled. The muses will come but with their faces blank as TV screens.

Poker-Face

Einstein sits in a church, hair foaming beneath his yarmulka, violin on his knee. What about violins makes even the physicist vocal? Is this the music we will hear at the end of the world above the hum and click of decaying atoms? You can almost see his hands just below the picture, heavy with their load of heat as if he knew the luthier finds the best wood only from trees struck by lightening. Some will give wood its turn to grieve. But he is tired, tired of filling the air with invisible strings, tired of Kafka, tired of this endless bitching about the long disease of his life. He should have known better than to fall in love with anyone called F. In the Cypress Hills at night, coyotes howl like children screaming, like violins tightening in the air.

10%

Ten months since her mother died. It was this time last year when the doctors told her she would live only a few months more. My friend talked to a woman the other day who said her mother had died the same way, her cells repeating the same dull routine until they could stand it no longer. When she tries to think of her, the memory fills with static. Her mother now lives in a red box on the living room table. "When they burnt her," she says, "they used a garden rake to gather her body in." There is a painting by Caravaggio of Thomas the Doubter staring straight ahead, almost blind, as his finger disappears into Christ's grey wound. Some passages you will only understand by going through them. "Thomas's faith in holes to disappear into," says Emily Dickenson in a letter, "was stronger than his faith in faith." There are days that make me want to enter life, completely. There are days I want to live only at the edge of things.

In This Damn Town, Even the Moon is New

Short of rolling papers, he smoked a manuscript one Russian winter. Words are always closest to fire. Kafka on his deathbed asking that his diaries be burnt, the blood in his head building a new typeface. The last words in his journal: "More than consolation is: You too have weapons." But this is the opposite—taking words into your lungs and not letting them out. If only they were so easily taken back and forgotten. She asked me to forget my plans, my writing, my one great work. We need a house, we need comfort, we need children. Felice said. Poor, poor Kafka, off in the corner trying to break his addiction to her, trying to end his reliance on pain. But his body hurt him. It was his one and only audience.

Just This One Last Time, I Promise

Laudanum, a mixture of alcohol and opium. Something about it and the seventeenth century made one a Romantic. You could wander for days in somnolent slumber. The poet Coleridge once employed a man whose sole job was to stand between him and any chemist from whom he could buy it. But nothing worked. He loved laudanum and woke from one dose to the next. A slight froth across the mind. Milk-white waves of the afternoon folded in his lap like paper.

Stolen Time

Glenn Gould, rough coughs, snorts, humms, articulations on the edge of sense.   If we were listening to opera, the baritone would be singing his grocery list,   tenderly.   It reminds me of hearing Mozart at Notre Dame the summer I moved to Montréal to study French.   Halfway through, a woman fainted—moved more by heat and pregnancy than passion—and four men rose to drag her out. The mound of her belly floating down the centre aisle, dark patches of sweat on her dress.   I remember little of what was played that night, yet the peripheries are unforgettable.   I sat beside a woman I would sleep with a year later and never hear from again. I remember how even music at the time bombarded my head like a foreign language.   And maybe the message is, listening to Gould, that it's not all about music but about the potential of silence.
How rests are written as notes with their own octaves and harmonics and this is memory's space.   The lungs and mind can't stop, they say, even if they wanted to but we, we can at least pause in our gambling.   As if somebody had gotten into the music and kept the door open and we see the engine room of a great machine.   It's about panic   about pain.   I am preparing you for death, the music whispers, here and here and here and here.

———————————————————

There and there and there and there. Nothing so good we cannot sadden it.

❧

Let the Horse Wander

. . . the horse was allowed to roam freely, followed by a band of soldiers. If the horse's progress was impeded, the king would fight for the land in question. The entire area over which the horse wandered in a prescribed period was taken to be the king's unchallenged territory, and the horse was slaughtered . . .

My pretty.
My sleek one.

One Good Draft Would Finish Him

"All you think of is poets," she said, "no wonder you get nothing of importance done."

Writing and erections were permanently linked for William Carlos Williams. Writing blocks were coincident with bouts of impotence. He was never happier or writing better than when sleeping around. *Poetry*, he said, *is a good fuck . . . and one that takes.* After several strokes, he retired from his paediatric position at the hospital. As a going-away present, the staff gave him a new electric typewriter. He liked it. It hummed so cleanly. His wife remembered the sound of him in his room upstairs, tapping. The sound we hear at the edge of the world. He fell in love, like most men, with the tab key.

Fetish

because winter light is thesaurus to the lonely

because bone bleached in sun has no need

because his sister drowned three months before—her body wrapped in weeds, mouth an inch below the surface—where now we walk

because the cold is children holding flashlights to their hands gazing at their illuminated bones

because sex in the snow at 42 below zero remains both tempting and lethal

because Emily Dickinson was once found in her parlour in the arms of a stranger

because every heart has a North West Passage that does not freeze or, if it does, is not broken

because, like Columbus with amnesia, I found you again

because light caught in morning frost moves not at the speed of light but with no speed at all

because, having tied the carcass to a fencepost, hunters wait in willow scrub for the wild dogs to come

because Acteon saw Diana / in the spring and I / saw nothing

because everything you do is in the past tense of everything you know

because we were not the doe found frozen beneath a drift of snow

because in German, *Scherz* (joke) is very close to *Schmerz* (pain)

because I don't know what to believe in anymore, don't know what believes in me

because a small boy in New York shot the last passenger pigeon with a pellet gun

because it's my poem, and I'll cry if I want to

because I could

because I could not

because, in purely thermodynamic terms, the body you love is a heat source

He Waits Until Tomorrow

"What can I do without him?" is the question passed down through my genes. My family has a history of being smitten with the worst people. Lines of alcoholics, debtors, farmers. There are reasons to tell him of my need and reasons to not. For: It is spring. For: It is like marriage and so another step towards failure. Against: Winter is the season for tears, they get lost in the snow flurry. Against: I think I can wait until tomorrow. It is the end of my orbit, my tether. I can hear the line of his ribs in darkness, curved as Ruskin would curve them, *like a bow just bent*. Hell, he never liked Ruskin anyway.

There is an Obvious Solution to Your Problem

Myth is only the repetition of story, of a joke so good you can't stop telling it. At the height of the Phrygian festival of Cybele, some men (moved by music and the shedding of blood) would castrate themselves, tearing away, as Catullus says, *the burden of their groin*. Castrates became the goddess's priests. When I was younger and worked on a farm, I castrated pigs in spring. With the legs spread wide, its head muffled in a burlap sack, I would make two small incisions between the legs and push the testicles, which hadn't descended yet, out through the slits of skin. With one quick pull and cut, I would toss them to the waiting dogs. Hundreds a day. It was like fixing machines. The fear of castration is not the fear of emasculation but the fear of becoming a *plaything*—capable of the act but not of the need that leads it. For what sex (even homosexual) is not made more consummate by the fear of *fertilization*, that I will pass *something* onto you? My fluid, my love, my sperm, my blood, my virus. *Potent*—from Latin, meaning *to have power*. *Potent*—from Middle English, meaning *crutch*.

Madame Marie Curie

I am burning up. Every night, I think of Felice's body beneath microscope. "I love you," she said, "down to your cell structure." I should have drawn her body in sleep and pasted the drawings in an empty room. Maybe it is not her I love, but this missing of her. Maybe she knows the secret, that the best part of being together is being alone. July, 1910. Kafka has just set down his pen. He has written for the second time in his diary, "I don't avoid people in order to live quietly, but rather in order to be able to die quietly." How good to survive even the smallest thing, he thinks, returning from Felice's house in the woods. How good to feel freed by the skill to feel nothing.

I Have Done This to Show What an Englishman Can Do

If you were, geographically, a Lesbian, where would your yearning be, he wonders? He has been thinking all day how to translate *my pain drips* back into ancient Greek. He has come close with "I want to sink into Felice, a burning coal in snow." The last lengths of light fall on the bed beside him—they have travelled so far to bring the world to his face. The scent of another woman still on his hands, his mouth, a turgid dampness, the pulse deep inside his tongue. "I believe in you, verb, adjective," he writes, "I believe in what you will do with the named." He holds the paper to the light and the light crumbles.

No, This is Not The Bat Cave

At the entrance to the cave, Eurydice half-smiles for the cameras, fixing her hair. "I don't know what happened," she says, grimacing from the TV screen, "but the next thing I know, I turn around and he's not there." She cries a little showing the bruise on her arm, "He was always like that, strung out to the far edges. You know, loving him was like renting land." She pauses to breathe and wipes mascara from her cheek.

"I'm real sorry," she says, looking at her watch, "but I have to leave now. Apparently, the quick brown fox is again jumping over the lazy dog and I'm expected to do something." She mutters something under her breath then turns back to the microphone, "The godly are stretched to the limit out here. I haven't slept in days—look at me." She crowds her face toward the camera, "I could carry hell under these eyes."

"But one last thing," she says, half turning away, "those rumours, ignore them. I still miss him and his fancy plucking, like any girl would."

The End of This Section

I think of Felice every day as I descend to sleep and words break down into the sounds I knew before anyone taught me meaning. If you disintegrate fast enough into slumber, you become the parts of Sappho we are missing. If you fall there because of a woman, you become the parts of Sappho we already have. Clear crisp lines of May. The start of summer and in poems even the boy whores wear flowers, but out there they don't. Only needle-tracked arms and dirty jeans. Nothing left of the night now but me and them and silence. Red corpse of the night. Red branches of dogwood and rain-sluiced paths, actually. Browning grasses. The people walking by my window and the darkness they disappear into, gladly.

III

Day and Night the Sea Whispered Thalassa

She called to say her mother had died
    earlier that day. In her voice there was
no quivering
    but solidity as from one who has found

the flaw in matter. Somewhere distant lilacs
    and purple thunderheads opening
over grasslands. The start of losing her
    was knowing what could be missed:

a movement of hand, snap-
    dragons in the window, a way
of occupying the gaps between the times
    she wasn't noticed—which are

lust, are presence, the one way time

finds its way home. She promised the day before
    she would soon get better and so
the start of fiction.
    I can't remember what I said

but it was unimportant
    —language coiled
in silence as, on the coast,
    small pieces of glass worn by the sea

are called "Angels' Tears" for we think grief
    the permanent state of the godly. Sitting in a room
with the afternoon light falling through the window—
    which was everything between you and what you

wanted to get at—her mother's body grew cold
   as love can, as a *thing* being written *about* can.
Flowers on the table dropping white
   petals to the pastel rug, not losing them

symbolically but, as in real life with real flowers, one

by one. How quiet
   stillness
waits yet how ceaselessly
   we pursue it. How quiet. How helpless.

A smell in the room not of
   death but of things to be remembered:
hair over forehead, an empty glass
   of water. There are few

times we appear human enough
   for paintings but death is one of them.
I *hope*, she said to me, her voice over the telephone
   distant, as from one side of a wound

to the other, I *hope*,—the syllables
   coming down from the wire, dis-
mantling, as if *they*
   and *soon* and *her*

were sounds of another language
   that would have to be washed,
dressed and put to flame, the words
   becoming the body lying there now

dismantling protein, now a certain thickness
   of light as it digs itself out of colour, now
the unbeknownst heroine of a story she is
   instrumental to yet not a part of, separating, separating . . .

As if something was leaving, was

building its own ending apart from all of us—
   the imprint on the sheets, the verbs cooling down
into nouns already, into the body, spirit and breath
   which the Incas would draw

as scrolls of paper hanging before us
   all rolling up into an ending, now, more complete than
even the end of words or breath which,
   especially now, with the light lost in trees and snap-

dragons stubbing themselves out in the window, where even the notes,
   the early evening dew on grass, the spirit rising
with the thermals from the sun-baked ground, even the sky
   which has fallen, is falling, will continue

to fall, even the crumpled pieces of paper
   sewn into the cuffs of jackets

(especially the crumpled pieces of paper sewn into the cuffs of jackets)

that Pascal called his *inimitable proof of god*, even that,
   burning off into denouement, into unending thrust, into funerals

and eulogies, into the cakes and sandwiches eaten
   after, after all, after that, after this, after
she said, *I hope*, and it need mean nothing more than
   itself, the simple need for finality, like one cleaning up

corn husks after a great meal, but it was more
   finished than even this or an ending could rightfully be,
I hope, she said to me over such long distance, *I hope*
   they soon come and get her.

Daybreak on 5th Street

Trying to avoid description
this morning too cold for words.
Grass stiff with last night's frost.
A woman across the street
in her balcony window
buttons the last buttons of her blouse.
She has practised work in her sleep.
Today, cleaning faeces from a patient
in intensive care, she will think
of the sunrise-blue
around the downtown towers.
The way she stands in the window
means she could go on fastening forever
if only it subtracted from the balance of labour.
This morning like the quiet rain
in Kurosawa's *Seven Samurai*
before the last battle.
A morning full of hooves
galloping through deciduous forests
which is the sound of bandits
cocky but unsure about death
by the hoes and rakes of peasants.
They will gallop through the village gates
one by one, in cinematic splendour
as if death counted them out.
As the last one falls
beneath the solemn-faced samurai
and is dragged through the dust
by his stirrups, the movie will fade
to burial mounds and the static grey
of a blank TV. The woman, her blouse

buttoned, tightens the belt around her skirt.
She is oblivious to old Japanese movies
because there is already too much
that needs. She eats porridge and cries
at the kitchen table. She doesn't know
what she thinks.

A Letter

Dear Dave,

Early frost and farmers gather the last
of summer wheat. We have gone through this
before, this surface of gleam
and brown-eyed wonder and the days
dragged us under. Days that remind me
of my mother mending jeans by winter light
at the kitchen table. A simple scene. No,
she is not the maid in *The Mistress and the Maid*
by Vermeer, but the one to the left of the painting
mending jeans. The maid does not see her
as if her work (moving from one pantleg
to the next) were past the edge of labour. The maid
holds a letter in chiaroscuro and easy lines
white as sheet lightning.
                         Today every act seems smaller
than the act that led it. Walking down to the creek
and surprising three bedded deer, their bodies
almost invisible, the colour of dried grass
and Russian thistle. How often
we have wished for such simple exchanges
passing the letter from one hand to the next
the message preserved in a kind of winter.
That there is time, still, to do so—stopping
by the creek, ache of cold in my hands as I reach
beneath the water surface to turn a stone.
The message will continue through the underbrush
and we will follow as far as the light allows.
An action not unlike—stone in hand—writing a letter
for the waiting maid. She will wait

a century at least, I think, for it is a long letter
full of much setting down of pen
and walking outside to the nearby creek.
It describes those places where the writing stops
and the real begins. It is describing your face
in afternoon light. A letter heavy with Russian themes
and Anglo-Saxon order. Here, then, we can wait
where all-that-is-good will reach us, where the secret
of the given is part of what we, if only for a moment
(hands touching the rock, katydids scurrying), are.
But were we built for it or only (the Maid's hand
reaching out not to the Mistress but to her letter)
for its dreaming?
                        Sun reflected in water. Machinery
working a clearcut downstream. Dave,
what are these scenes we come upon, walking
through the temple of things? Are they word,
paint, or the paths chance has led us to?

In the Museum
Guanajuato, Mexico

    At Positos 46, just south
        of the university,
Diego Rivera—famous
    Mexican muralist—
        was born. 1886. Dining table,

polished rosewood
    cabinetry, tiled floor, another bed
        filled with god. How
we remember the eminent
    through the mundane. How

        we praise them. The
traffic beyond the terrace
    is thinking too of how
        to go on.
If only it could wait

    for those times when life
        counts. The day sick
with heat. Everything pushed
    beyond itself
        by the small

sails of light.
    The guards have fallen
        asleep because it is
too much, at times, to tend
    to the real

        children, a wife, lunch
in a paper bag.

            Labour, they think, is not
                    an exchange
but something you sell

            yourself into. There are
                    paintings, for sure, drawings,
naturaleza
            muerta, etchings
                    humming in their frames, carrying

forward the innumerable
            details. Small eyes
                    skim the light
of its data. Up the stairs
            and to the left (don't

                    worry, I forgot my ticket
too) you can see a photo
            of the artist at work.
                    Tweed jacket. Brush held like a
cigarette. Paints on the pallet

            like bird shit. To the right,
                    in the photo, a female nude
holds a mirror to her face.
            She never bargained
                    on this

life that never ages
            and never moves—*what*
                    she wouldn't give
for something to lean on, you think.
            Slight glare of my eyes
                    in the glass watching
the stalled application of paint. And then

                there is you. And then
                        what is behind you
attending to the continual

                catch and release of the real.
                        Not that the dissection
only goes so far
        but there is no end
                once begun.

This prayer matter
        is praying. On the street below
                a woman sells postcards.
She stands contra-
        posto—hips skewed

                above her feet—and holds
the cards as if each repetition
        of the original hurt a little. Particle.
                Anti-particle.
Shade from an overhead

        tree. All of it merging
                into this one moment
of the true. O, how
        we want to help her
                across that gap

so much depends on.

Desires for Symmetry

When I think of you I think of bells
and an inner ear listens to the self
listening to the cathedrals that have right now
erected themselves within my hearing.
How the air grew tough and tenuous
as listening we were strung on fine threads
of attention. Even the cello dreams of breath-
ing the air inside the bell, that brassy significance
those open-bottomed lungs
whose breath is the blue world. As I turned,
I could feel in my spine the turning
of my mother, her mother, hers, each gong
going paddlestrokes back in time connecting us
by the need to observe this sounding order
its invisible flags through a god-soaked atmosphere.
And the scene feels instantly captured
by its accompanying tapestries. And the chimes,
spreading around the city now. And the
chimes, as if some creature had been woken
and its many hearts began to beat. And
the chimes, their brass thudding through the air
like a taste for meat. Memory raises
its congregational rows of cilia
which bend as I am now bending and rise
as I am now rising to you, this sound.

Embodiment

The contours of the room have taken them
to this beginning and they
are frightened of it, living on corners
where the world drops off.
They had not realized such simple touching
would lead them here, that the gaps
they had lived upon so long
would bring such pleasure.
His hand on a smoothness that reminds him
of nothing but his need to go further:
she is a hollow forming on the emptiness,
he is a whiteness the waves have left her with.
They have gotten into the ends of things
and don't know how to get out—
even the question takes them further.
Ice on the rain barrel outside, apples
husked by frost—anything to take their mind off it.
A radio somewhere plays The Lemonheads.
What word has her mind etched tonight
on this couch with him? What is he stroking
now, he can feel it, a newness
that diminishes and remakes his every entry
to this place, a taste like blackberries?
They are laying the meanings down, one by
one,
in something which has, as its reward,
no essence. This is the pleasure.
That they have somehow stepped beyond
the peripheries tying night to them,
tying tree to tree, coffee table
to coffee table. Their bodies mend

a small piece of the world and their hands
are its attendence. Outside,
the lines lead to a landscape
far beyond weather.
Their bodies combusted with use,
rimed with sweat and salt.
We will practice together, then, they think,
in this work and understand its splendour.
They move into each other and further
into it. There is no extremity.

In The Beginning, Pornography

They are so hesitant at first—
rising curve of rump and breastbone
subtle zippers and unbuttoning soft
genitals in cotton. They know so little
of each other but know so well
the quicker paths to what the body needs.
The photographer, his eye in the lens,
remembers salmon spawning in a river
not far from where he grew up.
Surge of river water, glitter
of scales and rock brimmed
with sperm and silt.
Those who had come could do nothing
to stop themselves and their long
migration from the highway, down
through the pine and willow scrub
to watch. They stood there
unmovable and quiet as the image
of the salmon swam deeper and deeper
through their brains.

He looks back through the camera.
Already someone's ribs are mottled
with semen, sprayed, unawares, by another.
It gathers like wet snow in October
as winter descends through mountain pines.
He thinks this and he thinks
how late the light this year
filling the room with faded yellows
and orange as if unmoored
from the day that carried it. Slight froth.

Slight scent of leaf rot.

The afternoon has already reached
a limit, but he has not stopped them.
For there is still everything
on the other side, wanting it
even more than they do.

Steam

        Driving from Montréal in the morning
smell of sleep still deep in the car, east
      to Québec City. The St. Lawrence blue and
        shifting below the Plains of Abraham
or whatever they call it now for the

      battle is still on (men rushing the steep
        banks, boats hidden below), interpreters,
speaking in soft Québécois, interpreting.
     Steam rises from the river, white, airy
        falling back over the rapids of itself

to be carried in the rising current
     of air—water throwing its anchor
        into the abyss again and again,
never tired of the trick—liquid then
     gas then liquid again—never tired

        of the unending spinning and respinning
of a name. It reminds me, sitting here,
     driving, of the steam we saw on the telecasts
from Chernobyl—white clouds above

     the concrete towers, scientists in lab coats
        with baffled worried faces stuck somewhere
between finding and making the anomaly.
     The camera panned to workers in lead suits
        heavy in the steam that whirled at their feet.

They will be dead in a year as will those
     in the nearby town

>   but for now they are
> part of the cloud that billows
>   back into itself, fallout rises
>
>   and twists to the wind-choked stratosphere.
>   It differs only in kind from the science show
>   I watched as a kid where they showed
> human copulation from the inside.
>   Vagina and erect penis moving in
>
>   and out of the camera angle, back and forth,
> walls red and pulsating on the TV
>   screen. It looked like nothing I had seen before,
>   penis, blurred and moving faster—bounced
> to the satellites and back—until even
>
>   the commentator went silent and a white
>   cloud arced through the liquid we did not even
> know we were in—white then clear then white again—
>   billowing through the picturetube and living
>   room and the vaginal walls coming down to force
>
> the last of the liquids out. Something was there, you could
>   feel it, something beyond
>   sex or childhood,
> ensuring the vital transfer
>   through the ionized air.
>
>   When it was done, the commentator
> resumed her even tones
>   and everything was science
>   and suspect again. Steam
> burns from the St. Lawrence now but something here wills

      the audit, some great mind wracked again and
          again on the edge of all it knows. Styrofoam
cups, chip bags, maple wood, the slower waves
    of bedrock. I am driving and thinking in the early
       morning because it is a world of analogy

and longed-for distance. I am thinking of steam
    because it is like memory and its
        relation to the real.
The river as quiet as history
    (the battle over, the messenger stuck

      in his eternity to get here—
which is exactly how long it should take).
    Joggers move through the paths which are part
      of the landscape which is
nothing again.

Tiger Lilies

What was lost in snow is now found
and we wish again we could lose it.
In my friend's voice, there was an eye
of grief her voice stepped through.
About one day walking into her room
to find her lover dead, his heart
exploded. It's too simple to say
something changed in her
but something did change—the way
in old paintings "depression"
is confused with "relief."

A figure falls from the sky
into an unnamed sea, ankles
miniature smokestacks above waves.
Seven willow branches hang heavy
with inked markings of snow.
We are centuries from gravity
and already we are learning
of weight. How a small boy
being fucked in the ass by his brother
beneath a willow tree
beneath summer green and slivered heat
thinks not of pain, submission or the fall of Rome
but crumblings in the language
that describes such things.
It is *being* as *falling*: his hands
braced against grass.
Another name, besides orange
and this light, for glory.

Mountain rivers, jade deep,
descend with rumbling
from snowpack in the Kootenays.

My body, all its tired utterances, at peace.

The rain tonight, skin warm
and wearing ankle bracelets, walks
through the room as we sleep.

Les Jeunes Filles Cueillent Les Fleurs
read for World AIDS Day, Calgary, 2000

A man shown in varying stages of undress
body piebald with shadow through venetian blind—
I have the tickets to take us there.
The scene-pack on easy wires and his body
gathering to meet us, as he said he would,
long ago, beneath the porch-lit ends of things
lit with hunger. Our coming traced
by the blue shift of going and
already we must think of the end
of our holiday here. The beach falls
through the harness of our luxury
and all the europeans have left us
with the luminous smell of river weeds.
If only we could go down to the sea
in ships again. If only we could hoist
so lightly our weapons. But we are so
tired by dying, "All my good friends
are gone" he said, "and all the gods are off
frisking the astronauts." But we have
memorized their stupid dactyls and
charming bigotry, what more do you want?
A mind where everything sounds like answers?
Like the headnote drying in the wind,
our scene will be harvested, the air invested
with seed as each alternative ache seeks out
another. T of collarbone. Y of buttocks
and thigh. The sound of someone softly
sawing a grapefruit. A mourning heavy as all the rest
with its load of hounds-tooth and plaid,
scented talcum and skin. And will we walk
equanimously then, dressed for the part

of the hired mourners? If each particular
took us away from the precision
of the ideal, will we ever find a chasm
deep enough for the medicines we need?
Retrovirals. Antiretrovirals. "Refineries
of the insatiable under the radicand of summer"—
it was his lachrymose words got us so depressed
in the first place. The horse-drawn charts.
You'll miss me when I'm gong. Gosh, this certitude
and any other rusted thing, I thought, seeing
your face in the red shift of gas light or beacon.
What else to say? In the winter, your body
ached for spring. In the spring, there was
always too much. There will always be too
many. Lost in the muzzle of chance. But the
waves fatten themselves on trash. But the night
makes noises like accordions falling. But we
have been undone and done back up again

∫

Octubre
for Rebecca Gowan

A man and a woman purposely avoid
the personal to get started.
She has not had sex in over a year.
The last time he had sex was with a man
half his age. Both carry that somewhere
in the space between them. The space their white
hands cross like arc welding on some tall metal
structure at night. It is night. Through
the window past his hands which are removing
her bra you can see the day crew leaving with
their lunch boxes. The night crew has returned
smelling like home and cheap soap. If we
were men there, we would understand
more the life of hands, how each tool
is a leap in the known. But his body
is thin and glabrous and reminds her
of the clear flesh of the cactus her mother
would cook. Her back striped with muscles
which jump beneath his hand. A phone rings
in a house nearby. A woman, she must
be in her seventies, answers it holding
the receiver upside down to her ear.
She hears nothing. She was unsure
about the new machines and now is less sure
and sets the receiver back in its cradle
where it will ring until morning. She sorts
dried red chillies on the table. The ones
that look like small withered breasts she will use
with roast pork. The smaller ones that look
like a man's penis in old age, she will mill
to a fine red powder. The words in Spanish

come to her easy as a light snow comes easy
in October and glazes unharvested wheat.
They feel the weight of the ungathered,
then, in the slow burn between them.
So much of the night unknown and they float
on that ignorance. Already they
are fucking and soon they will be crying.
The night held by such description. It
fans out over the abyss where it burns
and shines. Burns and shines.

Meditation on the Butterfly Sanctuary
Guadalajara, Mexico

                Therefore, we thought,
for a moment, we had it—the clarity
of an idea that fanned its wings, but now
it escapes beyond its intentions.
The roar of Avenida Indepencia
not even a block away, the sound
of buses crazed by the discovery of speed.
A man in a hospital room goes hungry.
He has AIDS and the orderlies
refuse to bring him food or enter his room.
Why not throw it all away, then,
the food, the sanctuary, the bloody trees?
Was its only use the drama of giving it up
in the first place?
Arrange flowers on a small wooden table.
Sell beauty products for a living.
Because thought is only gist
in solid state, nothing stops us
from the impossible or the insane.
And, at the moment you fall back
to yourself (another
gust of wind), you also fall away—
as a great pine will fall in the forest
the forester's muscles tensed
around the roaring machine.
And the air will be cooler there
as around the body of a dead thing.
And the wood will be fine grained and resinous.
And the sound of milling it will fill your afternoon.

Meditation on the Orchid Sanctuary
Guadalajara, Mexico

Orchids, you think, wandering
from one latinate tag to the next,
speak to each other in a language
of the dead. If you listen, you hear them
remembering names for actions
that don't happen anymore
to objects long disappeared.
Another argument, perhaps, for the end
of matter, the Beatles, god or something
bred so far past purity it feels dirty again.

But somebody has loved them well
For they have the air of wanting nothing
but empire, you suppose, or death
or a bit of life brought to them
in the afternoon. Each sucks its ounce
of rot like a flesh wound.
                                          Remnants
of a wedding party from the morning
scatter along the footpaths (for soon
there will be an end to romance
and a start to the mundane),
half-eaten lunches and doodles of children,
scuffed workboots of labourers on break.
Everything comes here wanting
another world different yet the same.
And the orchids are promising,
promising . . . bloodshed, perhaps,
or woodshed or whatever they do
in times like this
in places like these.

Moth Light

2 AM and the moths
crash the window
drinking light from glass.

Night noises distill from nightmare
        —coyotes outside reclassify
    garbage to another category
of hunger. Night owls
    drag the grass for deer mice
and voles   —trolleys in fog
        moaning through the lower soundwaves.

        I have dreamt of a man
    who pulled a phonograph needle
        across a woman's skin
    and thereby sung himself to sleep
        and of a man who lay beside me
and listened to the small rain
    of deer hooves
    across the polished lawns.
Dreams of insomnia
    enumeration of the possible
    where etc.
    finds its niche.

I turn on the reading lamp
    the moths smell it and come
        to fry their brains in light.
In the morning they will be nothing
        but husks
        on the hardwood floor

                        architectures of dust
                                    and pocket lint
            winged miscellany   part
                        of the total loss
            emptied of the fanatic juice
                                    that led them on.

One by one, they leave me here,
        nothing
                and in danger
        of becoming less
                                full
                of all the ballast they gave up
            departing for the chaste
                    cold seas of the moon.

Pieces

In the dent beside your body—
your hand curled by my chest
as if that were what
we have tried to reach
Your thighs
        heavy with night's pull
The way that sounds
              beside me

The edges of the window blur
every effort to see through it
has taken a piece of its clarity

Rooms thicken in their progress
through time
              Somewhere   a dog
                  at the end of a bed
in its country of sleep

Already, narratives unravel become
texture: the thing you did with a spoon
your friend drinking water in his sleep
telling us when he woke
he was most afraid of drowning
                                —visions
crawl back to the eye
              return
to the eaves

True   in *The Maltese Falcon*
I wanted to be the woman: arrested

                bathed in last camera light
                                        Seductress
and bitch
                to live the rest of her life in colour

Why did we never see her sleep?

I hear your body's private moans
where the new alphabets
are brewing

Now, there is no end
to the land before us

Now   there is

IV

holding pattern

"Don't cry whilst writing letters. The person receiving the letter is apt to take it as a reproach. Undefined misery is no use to anyone. Be clear, or, better still, be silent. If you must tell the world about your personal affairs, give examples. Don't just sob in the pillow hoping someone will overhear."

Mavis Gallant
A Fairly Good Time

Now begin that intensive year-long study on occurrences of gesticular arthritis in the saffron pickers of central Spain I've always wanted to do

go to bed every night and dream of his tongue gliding in and out of the cool lake of your mouth[1]

how the skin of two lovers knits together in an incomparable weave. A comparable weave. At last, we've something to compare

learn again how to sign all letters
                        Sincerely,[2]

pursue my life-long ambition as a closet lepidopterist[3]

try not to think of the fine brown hair on your stomach when wiping moth dust from the rim of my glasses

pursue a mathematics of one

---

[1] Who penetrates whom here? The oceans are not always calm. The waves that lap the shore can be tidal waves.

[2] The poem reveals its evolutionary weakness. Originally, this line read: "get that lobotomy and nuclear arsenal / I've always wanted to do." The performative mentality of this—especially the ungrammatical switch from "get" to "do"—clearly, and cleverly, rules.

[3] Much of *Lolita* was written while collecting butterflies. Nabokov swore to his death his facility with English was lacking. There is a picture of him as a boy, he in the middle holding onto his parents like wings.

I only
thought
of you
once
boarding
the plane again
and again and
again[1]

recross the Empty Quarter in heels, carrying a photograph of John Thompson. Deny the "stunt quality" of the journey[2]

avoid bestial thoughts[3]

try not to think of your hands skating over his ice of nerves[4] / your wonder at finding one of his hairs in your mouth in the mid-afternoon / the taste of your blood in his / try not to think / just

watch the sun pour through the window / splattering the walls with yolk

construct a blank globe and start over[5] (in so doing, postulate that the mind is a sentimental creature)

---

[1] Notice how the "o"s are slowly—as if in a receding alphabetical tide—replaced by the small case "i"s and the audible "a," "a," "a." Impotence rears its audible head.

[2] Wilfred Thesinger would surely beat the crap out of me for that one.

[3] Implying, of course, there are bestial thoughts to avoid already. The tail wags the dog. Basements form the structure.

[4] Hockey, more than a national pastime, is a passion. How often has a game of pick-up turned into something else, altogether?

[5] Like Columbus with amnesia, only to discover you again. (I can't remember, have I used this line already?)

realize again why so very little can honestly begin
Dear beloved,[1]

publish a cantankerous paper on loneliness as an evolutionary leap in the construction of hollow bones. Seek government funding[2]

calculate how many mammals die / each hour making time / go on its way

think nothing of how I collected your nail clippings with the avarice of selenographers[3]

contemplate how last fall / when the air bled on the trees / how you slept beside me / in your boy's body

think nothing of your ears uncurling into your brain in elaborate fiddleheads

try not to think, just[4]

your sweat / sweet salt[5]

visit the zoo and attempt to release bats. If unsuccessful, return home and reread *The Hairy Ape*

---

[1] Dear Beloved,   Dear Beloved,   Dear Beloved,
    You asshole   Your plums in the freezer   I should have known

[2] Perhaps no man seems so lonely as he who must project. The ships come in. The ships go out. Today, a protest in Japan over a cruiser in port carrying nuclear weapons. The protest was stifled. There are few reasons, the government assured, to worry.
    Jubilation in the streets.

[3] Pointing with a finger (nail like a piece of horn) and said, "Look, the moon."
    The Sea of Solitude.
    (the blue-veined wrist)

[4] The poet believes by constructing holes, he will be holy.

[5] Philtres made of the beloved's bath water. Isles unknown to the heart's geese.

stage Hamlet with an entourage of hamsters

just pretend I didn't eat the damned pomegranate ('*quos ego Persephonea maxima dona feram*'—but writing yourself into hell makes not a hero of you, poet)[1]

lost love / a petty sorrow of the privileged / born of boredom both 'exquisite and / excessive'   or   how much harder would this be while waiting tables

become the man who measures the annual rainfall on the Serengetti or Upper Amazon. If possible, communicate only by fax

make passes at every checkout boy I see and, if beaten, blame the whole thing on Allen Ginsberg and Walt Whitman[2]

promise to answer every telephone call with 'What fresh hell is this?'—accordingly, cite Dorothy Parker

curl around the blade of my abstinence[3]

try not to think of your dog's initial surprise at seeing him instead of me eating graham crackers naked by the light of the fridge, brushing stray crumbs from his hair[4]

ask Goldie Hawn out for a date. Promise to buy her freesia

at first, be overjoyed I am out of the couples' commercial market but, on further study, be depressed by the fact I am now expected to buy my own cologne[5]

---

[1] And it makes not a Latinist of you either! The poet's status as bogus intellectual is revealed. He is hailed in the streets as a revolutionary simpleton. He prances naked on a white stallion, calling all the women by name.

[2] Ginsberg died shortly after this was written. I had sent him no letters for months. He died, though in a crowd of mourners, of my solitude.

[3] What, exactly, do you whittle? The curls represent those on a man's chest. The blade has just cut onions for the eyes that cry in the pan.

[4] I like the manliness of this piece.

[5] These lines stink. In his hand, he held his genitals, an unexpected bouquet. Musk. Fresh duran.

become a waiter and, after gaining the respect of my employer, one day offer fresh trilobite as lunch special to unsuspecting patrons of the *nouveau cuisine*

call this a "tactic"[1]

think nothing of your complicated clumsiness / how you lost contact lenses with an unmatchable perfection / how banging your head was at times lyrical, poetic / how the door catching your hand / began my only novel[2]

again wonder why I cleaned up after your stupid Christmas party when you left only days later. Not that I'm bitter / just wish I had requested a decent hourly wage

Eurydice asked, "And love, where are you leading me now?"[3]

contemplate *what truth is it that makes men so miserable*. Under the auspices of a feminist reinterpretation, apply for government funding[4]

---

[1] I write these words in salt.

[2] My song is deep in the ink. Here the poet thinks himself much more productive than he is. The novel, incidentally, was scrapped shortly after. The poet pretends he has been writing under the pseudonym "George Bowering" for years.

[3] We were at the corner of 4th and 5th. Looking back on it now, I see myself looking back.

Orpheus looked back for he was filled with nostalgia. His turning was an act of memory, a fleeting glimpse of the past in the present, before she fell back again. But for a second, longing had allowed her memory to follow.

Or did Orpheus carry at his back a mirror, so, turning, all he saw was his own image turning to view him? Seeing it, he fell down, in love with himself?.

Lesson: don't look, don't question, love will follow—but like a shadow.

[4] (Jubilation in the streets.)

search for the sound a tonotopic map of your body would produce
so, once this sound is heard, your exact picture would appear in my
auditory cortex. Be justified in throwing out your pictures[1]

    your face a
    closed door a   *and know this*
                                               whoever you
    couplet a   *will love*
    complete a

    final a[2]   *of the arrows*[3]
                                                      Sappho

you, sleeping in your boy's body[4]

telephone my mother and tell her I'm the son-of-a-bitch who left
home and time her responses in hanging up knowing if they
become progressively better at least she's not dying[5]

ask checkout girls where I could find a date. Make bad puns about
bagging while brushing hair from my eyes, innocent-like[6]

"Isotope" in white block letters across his shirt.

---

[1] When the US tested its first hydrogen bomb (Mike) on the island of Elugelab on the Eniwetok Atoll in 1952, the test was confirmed around the world by slight needle quivers on seismic recorders.

[2] "ou," "a," "a," "o," "oo," "a," "ou," "a," "o," "a," "a," "a." The poet catches himself at the height of passion. The horizon speckled with beluga whales.

[3] *"you make me hot / I gave you a white goat."*

[4] Gender as a coat which our mothers force us to wear. The boy will appear repeatedly as a motif. I send him *you* to woo *him*.

[5] It was a transgender line. *Hello? Hello?*

[6] The grocery store may well be the poem's true setting. Persephone, holding a pomegranate, asks the clerk, "How long? How often?"

it became progressively obvious that what she meant by "manned" was by someone other than me

cover my living room floor in papadums and dance barefoot to the sarangi until a fine dust coats the walls

wonder if the mind can metamorphose into something greater by forgetting all that has come before it. Does the moth forget the larva and, if not, does this memory haunt it?

consider every night not a seam / but a break[1]

beat myself and throw my case at the pity of the lower courts

believe that though we never took pictures of our fucking this had no real reflection on its integral "goodness"[2]

how I used to call it 'lovemaking'[3]

gather wooden spoons around me, to shore myself against my ruin[4]

try not to think, just

---

[1] Death. That was a death sentence.

[2] There were pictures though. I showed them to dirty old men and made them weep.

[3] Those who went up in the balloon were never heard from again. In the report, the inspector wrote, "another mystery descends."

[4] There is no justice in love. Only the unjust survive it:
  The night came in armour.
    The knight came in amour.

you, sleeping in[1]

build an elaborate narrative which proves this to be the best action for both of us yet denies "this" actually happened[2]

try to avoid the use of that word "both"

reread the Song of Songs on purely allegorical levels

place a world map on an overhead projector and position myself so the Sudan falls slightly right of my navel. Call myself "Continental"

such an extraordinary thing / a woman stirring a blue pot // ah

buy a goldfish and rename it Herodotus then implore him, pleadingly, to shut up

wish I had recorded the sound of a phonograph needle sliding across your skin so I might now describe the exact process of its construction[3]

avoid the use of that word "love"

---

[1] In what, dammit? Thongs made of harp strings? Virgin wool? Rapping the gavel, the statues refused to speak.

[2] The past rises in and out of memory like whales surfacing for air.
    Rilke was right, *be ahead of all parting.*

[3] Scientists have prevented whales from beaching by playing whalesongs far out at sea. Transference is as strong as any original seduction. Sometimes the sound of a wave is a wave, but drier.

       errant
       eros

       a rose
       arisen[1]

you, sleeping
in your coat of phoenician red (your face / bruised by sleep)[2]

contemplate how an empty room containing a jazz musician is still an empty room[3]

there of, there of[4]

start a mail-order "poet kit" featuring goatee trimming tools, a cheap beret or, alternately, black hair dye and a pair of ripped tights

sell apocryphal mining shares to my friends and family

it was winter
Brueghel *was not right*

---

[1] Every commercial I have appeared in has typecast me as a slut. Some nights—though very few, it is true—there are reasons for sleeping alone. Couples seem natural, nuclear, atomic. (Jubilation in the streets.)

[2] It is said the daughters of Mnemosyne would bathe in pools of pure blue reason. *The woman's blood should be kept in vials.*

[3] A case in point: Contemplate how every room . . . is still an empty room.

[4] Winters in Alberta. Hoar frost falling from the trees.
    Icharus flying into the atom, wings melting.
    His spiral path through the cloud chamber.

of there of here
of her of he
of h of[1]

why every poem must be as ugly and twisted / why one voice just isn't enough[2]

sleep with a doll playfully named Richard Strauss / the String Quartet #2 in C minor painting the background

you,[3]

when you left our breath hung in the air as if the very weather was exhausted with us. You closed the taxi door, brushing snow from your boots, and the day fell finally into place / when I turned away / every piece of glass[4]

> This is a difficult piece with complex harmonies and counterpoint and yet it maintains a deep, intense and compensating lyricism through-out. Now . . . Glenn Gould's String Quartet, Opus 1   CBC, August 18, 1997[5]

if there is pleasure in pain, why call it pain

---

[1] Perhaps the reverse is just as revealing:

    e
   re
  ere
 here
there

[2] Schizophrenia, though common in the family . . .

[3] When I picture you, I lose bits of your body. More and more is replaced by blanks, pieces of white space, dark caves of absence. Soon, there will only be a negative and you will walk behind me—but as a shadow.

[4] Please, poet, we beg you to keep your bourgeois fatalism to your melodramatic self. This is no place for empty gesturing. This is so eighties.

[5] Toronto here functions as the edge of my loathing, where Canada ceases to be geographical but becomes an osmological frontier. The death, I repeat, of poetry.

I held you after your morning shower and your tears stained my
shirt a bluer blue. I still believe this required no strength at all[1]

> Things
>   come and go
> Then
>   let them
>   Creeley

yes, yes but the man *actually* played a blue guitar[2]

see, love, how each of these days are for you

---

[1] Sometimes, what draws us together keeps us apart. Nuclear forces / of the heart.

[2] This was spoken by a woman in Fredericton, NB in the winter of 1997. We had each had several pints of beer and would have several more before we were drunk enough to screw. There was a band playing. She whispered in my ear.

SHANE RHODES has published poetry, reviews, articles and essays in magazines and newspapers across Canada. He has been an editor with The Fiddlehead, filling Station and Qwerty. His first book of poetry, The Wireless Room, won the Alfred G. Bailey Award for Poetry and the Alberta Book Award for Poetry in 2000. Holding Pattern was written while living in Mexico and Canada.